Parasites & Partners

HITCHERS AND THIEVES

Kieren Pitts

Raintree

Chicago, Illinois

D1537345

Raintree

Chicago, Illinois

First published 2003 by Raintree, a division of Reed Elsevier Inc.
© 2003 The Brown Reference Group plc

All rights reserved. No part of this book may be used or reproduced in
any manner whatsoever or transmitted in any form or by any means, electronic
or mechanical, including photocopying, recording, or any information storage
and retrieval system, without written permission from the copyright owner
except in the case of brief quotations embodied in critical articles and reviews.
For information, address the publisher:
Raintree, 100 N. LaSalle, Suite 1200, Chicago, IL 60602

Library of Congress Cataloging-in-Publication Data

Pitts, Kieren.
  Hitchers and thieves / Kieren Pitts.
     p. cm. — (Parasites and partners)
Summary: A comprehensive look at different types of creatures that ride
on larger, more active animals in order to find food or mates, or simply
to travel long distances.
Includes bibliographical references (p.   ).
  ISBN 0-7398-6989-2 (lib. bdg. : hardcover) — ISBN 1-4109-0356-7 (pbk.)
  1. Phoresy—Juvenile literature. [1. Symbiosis. 2. Animals.] I.
Title. II. Series.
  QH548.P58 2003
  591.7'85—dc21

                          2003004227

ISBN 1-4109-0356-7

Printed and bound in Singapore.
1 2 3 4 5 6 7 8 9 0 07 06 05 04 03 02

Acknowledgements

The publisher would like to thank the following for permission to use photographs:

Key: l – left, r – right, c – center, t – top, b – bottom.
Ardea: Jean-Paul Ferrero 22, Pascal Geotgheluck 28, P. Morris 8; **Raphael Carter:** 10b; **Corbis:** Michael & Patricia Fogden 17b,
Peter Johnson 5t, Jeffrey L. Rotman 5c, Tim Zurowski 30; **John Hafernik:** 5b, 16, 17t; **Jeff Jeffords:** 4cb; **Steve Marshall:** 4b, 15, 18,
23t, 24, 25, 26b, 27b; **Natural Science Photos:** W. Cane 26t, Steve Downer 10t, Richard Revels 27t; **NHPA:** Stephen Dalton 13b,
Paal Hermansen 21, T. Kitchin & V. Hurst 9b, Christophe Ratier 29b, Norbert Wu 7; **Oxford Scientific Films:** 9t, Tui De Roy 23b,
Konrad Wothe 13t; **Photodisc:** Alan & Sandy Carey 29t, Photolink 4ct; **USDA/ARS:** Jack Dykinga 4t; **Front Cover: Steve
Marshall** (t); **Raphael Carter** (b).

For The Brown Reference Group plc

Project Editor: Jim Martin
Consultancy Board: Dr. Robert S. Anderson,
    Royal Canadian Museum of Nature, Ottawa, Canada;
    Prof. Marilyn Scott, Institute of Parasitology,
    McGill University, Montreal, Canada
Designed by: Pewter Design Associates
Illustrator: Mike Woods
Picture Researcher: Helen Simm
Managing Editor: Bridget Giles
Art Director: Dave Goodman
Production Director: Alastair Gourlay

For Raintree

Editor: Jim Schneider
Managing Editor: Jamie West
Production Manager: Brian Suderski

Front cover: A jackal fly feeds on the mixture of saliva
and digested organs dribbling down the head of a
predatory robber fly (*top*); a carrion beetle carrying
helpful mites (*bottom*).

Title page: Flower mites scamper toward the nostrils
of a feeding ruby-throated hummingbird.

Note to the Reader
Some words are shown in bold, like **this.** You can find out what they mean by looking in "Words to Know."

Parasites & Partners
HITCHERS AND THIEVES

Contents

Introduction

Animals and plants do not live alone. They are always interacting with other creatures. A close association between different species is called a **symbiosis.** *Parasites & Partners* introduces you to symbiotic relationships. You can see examples of these around you every day. Anyone who keeps a dog shares a symbiosis with their pet. The dog is fed and housed by its owner, who gains a companion and protection in return. Both partners in this relationship benefit, but that is not always the case. The different types of symbioses covered in this book are discussed in the box below.

Each book in *Parasites & Partners* looks at a different group of relationships. Find out how plants and animals interact with other types of creatures as they feed, breed, keep clean, find a home, and move around.

4

Some important words for you to remember

Symbiosis
A relationship between two different types of creatures is called a symbiosis. This bee is taking nectar from the flower to feed its young, while the plant is using the bee to spread its pollen. Both partners benefit in this example.

Mutualism
Biologists call a relationship where both partners benefit a **mutualism.** Clark's nutcracker eats pine tree seeds and buries stores of them underground to help it survive the winter. This helps the pine trees spread through the forest.

Commensalism
A relationship in which one **organism** benefits but the other neither profits nor suffers is called a **commensalism.** One of the partners is usually called a **host.** Here, a crinoid shrimp blends in with the colors of its feather star host.

Kleptoparasite
An animal that steals food from another is called a **kleptoparasite.** Their victims are called hosts. The tiny jackal fly on this praying mantis's eye will wander down its head to steal a bit of food.

▶ *These lions have driven a pack of brown hyenas away from a kill. Learn more about food snatchers on pages 20–29.*

◀ *Two remoras hitch a ride on a large humpbacked wrasse. Check out other animal hitchhikers on pages 6–13.*

5

In **this** book...

...you will learn about animals that profit from the work of others. In chapter one, find out about animals that get from place to place by hitching a ride on larger creatures. The animal that flies or walks from place to place is generally unaffected, but the hitcher enjoys free travel.

Sometimes, the relationship between hitcher and carrier is less amicable. The sinister hitchers in chapter two may eat their host's babies or steal their food. In the final chapter, discover how many animals do not go to the trouble of catching their own food but steal it from others instead. Many of these animal thieves are tiny, but some large creatures, such as lions and vultures, are expert food snatchers, too.

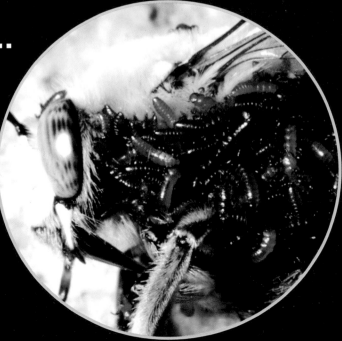

▲ *Young blister beetles crowd on to a confused male bee. Discover the world of sinister hitchers on pages 14–19.*

Hitching a RIDE

Many small animals cannot travel long distances to find food or a mate, but some get around by using a secret taxi service. They hitch a ride on larger, more active animals. The small animals get free trips to places they could never reach on their own.

6

Hitching a ride on another animal is called **phoresy.** Many species (types) of animals use phoresy to move to new areas, to find food, or to scatter their eggs. The animal used for transport is called the **host.** While the hitcher benefits, the host is unaffected and is often unaware of its passenger. Biologists call a relationship like this a **commensalism.**

Slippery suckers

One of the best-known groups of animal hitchhikers is the suckerfish. Suckerfish live in warm seas around the world. They hitch rides on whales, large fish, turtles, and even ships! Their slender bodies are usually white, gray, or stripy. Some species grow up to 3 feet (91 cm) long, and all have an oval sucking disk on top of their heads.

When a suckerfish finds a host, it swims alongside it. The fish attaches itself by squashing the sucker against the body of the host. The suckerfish then hitches a ride to new feeding grounds. It will sometimes hide from **predators** by attaching itself under the host.

▼ *A suckerfish hitches a ride on a much larger Caribbean reef shark.*

Scrap snatchers

The host provides a good place from which suckerfish can swim out to catch smaller underwater animals. Suckerfish often attach to the bodies of sharks. They steal scraps of food as the shark feeds. Biologists have also found small parasites in suckerfish stomachs. This suggests that the fish eat parasites on their host's skin.

Ship stoppers

Suckerfish are sometimes called remoras; *remora* means "delay" or "hindrance" in Latin. The fish were given this name because long ago people thought suckerfish slowed ships. A suckerfish is said to have attached itself to a ship belonging to the Roman emperor Caligula. Despite the efforts of hundreds of oarsmen, the ship could not be moved with the suckerfish attached.

Suckerfish are not always a hindrance. In China, Japan, and the Caribbean they were once used by fishers. Captured suckerfish were tied to fishing lines and then released into the sea. People would wait for the suckerfish to attach to a turtle or a large fish. The fishers would then haul in both the suckerfish and its host.

Salamander transport

Many other underwater creatures use larger creatures to help them get around. The red leech is a

▲ *A suckerfish uses the powerful sucker on its head to attach to other animals.*

type of worm common in fresh waters in North America. It moves to new areas by attaching to one of the front legs of a male spotted salamander. The leech also benefits from scraps of food discarded by the salamander.

Flying false scorpions

It is not just underwater animals that use phoresy to get around. False scorpions are a group of **arachnids**—relatives of animals like ticks and spiders. False scorpions are very common but are rarely seen since most are less than 0.2 inches (5 mm) long and live in moss, dung, or

◀ *This tiny false scorpion is hitching a ride on a fly by clinging to its wing.*

▼ *Red leeches hitch rides on spotted salamanders like this one. The leeches prefer male salamanders, since the females are more likely to die during the breeding season.*

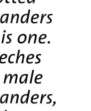

9

under bark or fallen leaves. They look a little like real scorpions but do not have a long tail or stinger. Instead, they use a pair of pincers to catch tiny animals such as insects and mites to eat.

Despite being able to run backward as fast as they can run forward, false scorpions are too small to travel long distances quickly without assistance. So false scorpions use their pincers to hang onto insects, spiders, and even birds. During the summer and fall, for example, some false scorpions hang onto the legs or wings of houseflies. When the housefly lands in a suitable place, the hitcher releases its grip and jumps off.

Some false scorpions even hitch a ride safe beneath the hard wing cases of beetles! The wing cases protect the false scorpion, which eats tiny mites that live on the beetle's body.

Food and favors

Most hitching animals do not affect the animals that carry them. But sometimes hitchers and hosts form close associations that are of benefit to both partners—biologists call these relationships **mutualisms.** Some carrion beetles bury the **carcasses** (dead bodies) of small animals such as mice. A carcass provides a safe underground food supply for the beetles' flesh-eating young.

Before the burial is complete, though, flies and other types of beetles lay their eggs on the corpse. These rival insect **larvae** (young) would compete with the growing carrion beetles for food. However, several species of mites hitch a ride on adult carrion beetles. When the beetles reach a carcass, the mites clamber off their ride and eat any eggs already laid on the carcass. Once the job is done, the carrion beetles lay their eggs. The mites get a free ride to a good source of food, while the young carrion beetles are more likely to survive since any competing insects have been eaten by the mites.

▲ *A carrion beetle inspects the rotting carcass of a wood mouse.*

▲ *Helpful mites form clusters on the body of a carrion beetle.*

Hitching on hummers

Not all hitchhikers are happy to be taken wherever their host goes. Some animals need to be taken to very specific places and must make sure they only leave their ride at the right stop. Flower mites are tiny animals. Each species of flower mite feeds on nectar and pollen from just one type of plant. When the plant stops flowering the mites must move on. The mites rely on hummingbirds to transport them between flowers. When a hummingbird stops to feed at a flower, the mites charge up the bird's bill and climb into its nostrils. Several different species of mites can ride in the bird's nostrils at the same time, but usually no more than ten mites are carried by the bird.

When the hummingbird stops at the right kind of flower, the flower's perfume enters the nostril of the bird. This is the mites' cue to leave. They dash down the bill and into the flower.

mites

◀ *Flower mites dash up a ruby-throated hummingbird's bill as it feeds on nectar.*

11

Free-ranging eggs
Some animals use other animals as a delivery service. One of the most common deliveries is another animal's eggs. Human botflies are large, bluish-black flies that live in Central and South America. Their larvae develop under the skin of warm-blooded animals, including people, where they feed on the host's flesh. However, the adult human botfly is a noisy flier. Its loud buzzing would alert a host that a botfly was closing in. So, to get its young to a host, the human botfly uses sneaky tactics instead.

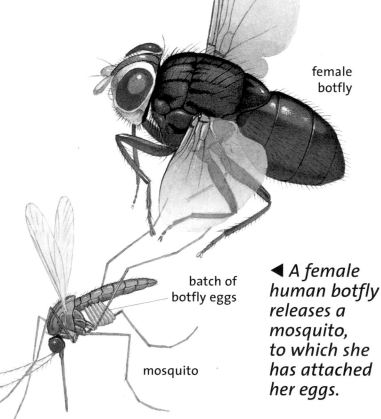

female botfly

batch of botfly eggs

mosquito

◀ *A female human botfly releases a mosquito, to which she has attached her eggs.*

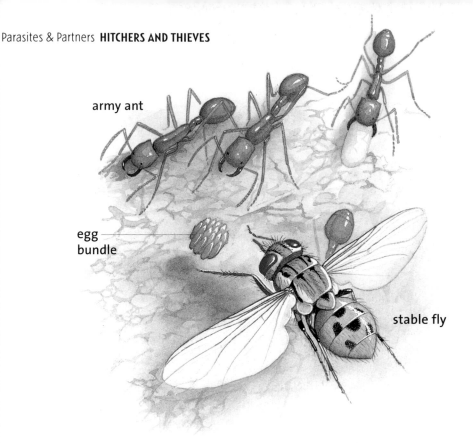

army ant

egg
bundle

stable fly

◄ This female stable fly is hovering above a trail of army ants. She has launched a bundle of eggs toward an ant, which will carry them to its bivouac.

12

Rather than flying directly to a host, a female human botfly captures a bloodsucking insect, usually a mosquito, in midair. The botfly attaches up to 40 eggs to the mosquito's body before releasing it. When the mosquito lands on a warm-blooded animal to feed, the botfly eggs quickly hatch. The larvae then burrow down into the host's skin.

Egg throwers

Getting eggs to a host can be a dangerous business. The larvae of an east African stable fly feed on scraps of discarded food in the temporary nests, or **bivouacs,** of army ants. But getting the young to the bivouac is tricky: army ants are ferocious **predators** that quickly grab and dismember

the adult flies if they can. To avoid the powerful mouthparts of the ants, an adult female stable fly uses stealth.

The stable fly hovers with a bundle of eggs above a column of **foraging** ants. She throws her egg bundle so it lands close to a worker ant. Thinking it is food, the ant picks up the egg

KEY FACTS

■ After capturing a smaller carrier insect such as a mosquito, a female human botfly carefully measures its size. The larger the mosquito, the more eggs the botfly attaches to it.

■ Human botfly maggots can wriggle through clothes to get to the skin of a person.

■ Only female false scorpions hitch a ride on the bodies of other animals; males stay put.

◀ *A tiny bird louse wanders through a forest of robin feathers. Bird lice can be fussy eaters and may only be able to feed on one species of bird.*

bundle and carries it back to the bivouac. There, the eggs quickly hatch and the larvae feed and grow.

Host hopping

Although it has many benefits in terms of saving time and energy, phoresy can often be risky. Bird lice are wingless **parasitic** insects that eat tiny fragments of bird feathers. Bird lice often live on just one type of bird. The lice usually pass between hosts while the birds are mating. But they can also spread by hitching a ride on blood-sucking insects called louse flies, which visit birds' nests.

Louse flies fly from nest to nest in search of new hosts. This can be bad news for the hitchhiking

bird lice. The louse flies feed on many species of birds, so the bird lice are often taken to unsuitable hosts, where they are unable to feed. These unfortunate lice must quickly find another louse fly to escape on or they will starve.

▼ *A louse fly drinks the blood of birds and can carry bird lice between hosts.*

13

Sinister **HITCHERS**

Not all hitchhiking animals are just along for the ride. Some use their taxi service as a source of food or a sneaky way to get into the nests of their hosts. These sinister hitchers are the reason why many animals must be careful about which passengers they pick up.

14

The young of other animals are an easy catch for many hungry creatures. Parents will go to great lengths to hide their offspring from these enemies. So, for a baby-eating hitchhiker, there is nothing better than being taken directly to the young animals by their unwitting parents.

Beastly baby eaters

The Costa Rica owl butterfly is a very large tropical butterfly with a wingspan of more than 7.5 inches (20 cm). This butterfly is named for the striking eyespots on the underside of its wings that make it look like an owl. A tiny chalcid wasp hitches a ride on an adult female butterfly. The wasp waits patiently until the butterfly lays her eggs. The little wasp then leaves its **host** and attacks the eggs.

The wasp lays eggs of its own inside the butterfly eggs before they have time to harden. The wasp **larvae** hatch and begin to eat the butterfly caterpillars before they can complete their development inside the egg.

Many other chalcid wasps wait on their hosts for a while before attacking the host's

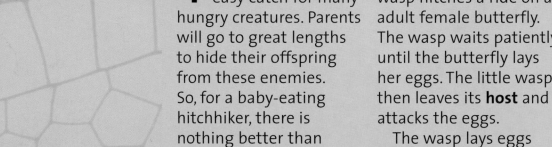

▲ *As this robber fly feasts on a beetle, it is joined for dinner by a tiny jackal fly that lives between the robber fly's wings.*

mantis

chalcid
wasp

ootheca

16

▶ *A tiny
chalcid wasp
wanders
down the
body of a
praying
mantis. The
wasp will lay
eggs inside
the mantis's
ootheca, or
egg case.*

▶ *These
blister beetle
larvae have
gathered into
a shape that
resembles a
female bee.
Would the
beetles fool
you, too?*

young. One species (type) of
chalcid wasp has hooks on its
legs. The wasp uses the hooks
to cling to the wings of female
praying mantises.

Mantises leave bundles of
eggs on twigs and stems, safe
in a papery brown case called
an **ootheca.** When the mantis
begins to produce an ootheca,
the wasp quickly scurries down
its body. The wasp then enters
the ootheca before it begins
to harden and lays her eggs
inside the mantis eggs. After
they hatch, the wasp's young
devour the growing mantises.

Getting from A to Bee

Blister beetles are large black or
brown beetles that live all around
the world. The young of most
blister beetles live as parasites
in the nests of bees. When they
hatch, the beetle larvae are fast
moving and agile, with hooks on
their legs. Most larvae wait on a
flower for a **foraging** bee to land.
They use the hooks to attach
themselves to the bee, and
are taken back to its nest.

Rather than wait for a bee to
visit a flower, the young of one
species of blister beetle go out
of their way to attract bees.
A group of these beetle
larvae gather together
and form a shape that
resembles a female
solitary bee. They also
release a chemical that
attracts male bees.
When a male bee lands
to investigate, the
beetle larvae
quickly
swarm over
him. They
attach
themselves
to his body
with the
hooks on
their legs.
They then
hitch a ride on
the male bee
until he succeeds
in finding a genuine
female bee.

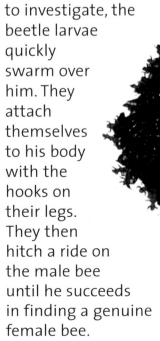

While the bees mate, the beetle larvae leave the male bee and climb onto the female. The female bee then carries the larvae back to its nest. Once they are safely installed inside the nest, the beetle larvae begin to feed on the bee's eggs.

Older, slower, and fatter

As the beetle larvae grow older, they become fatter and less mobile, and their legs become short and stumpy. They also stop eating the bee's eggs and instead begin to feed on its stores of **nectar** and **pollen.**

The beetle larvae stay in the bee's nest until they have **pupated** (turned into adults). Most blister beetles leave the nest soon after becoming adult, although some species continue living with their bee hosts.

▲ *These blister beetle larvae have managed to successfully hitch a ride on a confused male bee.*

◀ *An adult blister beetle's bright colors serve as a warning to enemies that it can release powerful defensive chemicals.*

◀ *Tiny flies gather on a dung beetle. The flies will mate on the beetle's back, and the females will lay eggs in a dung ball. The fly larvae will steal food meant for the young beetle larva.*

18

Fun with dung

Some insect hitchers take a ride so their young can steal all the food they need as they develop. Many dung beetles gather balls of dung and bury them. The female then lays an egg inside, and the larva feeds on the dung.

Certain tiny flies search out these dung beetles. They live on a beetle's wing cases and mate there. When a pair of beetles make a ball of dung, the flies wander down and lay their own eggs on it. The fly larvae compete with the young beetle for food. One species of small dung beetle hitches a ride

for similar reasons. The beetles live inside the shells of large land snails. This guarantees a constant supply of snail droppings on which the beetles lay their eggs.

Carrying food snatchers

Rather than hitching a ride to feast on a host's young or so their young can take their food, some flies steal the food of their hosts instead. Robber flies are fast-flying **predators** that hunt and catch other insects in midair. After catching their **prey,** they pierce its body with their sharp mouthparts and squirt digestive juices inside. These fluids dissolve

The cannibal run

Mantispids are unusual insects related to lacewings. Their young feed and develop inside the egg sacs of spiders, but finding these sacs can be tricky. Some mantispids avoid this problem through stealth. They stand upright on the tip of their body, before jumping onto a passing spider.

Once safely on board, the mantispid feeds on spider blood. For a spider, the worst enemy it can face is another, larger spider. Many are caught and killed by members of their own species. A **cannibalized** spider is no use for a mantispid. If it senses that its host is dead and is being eaten, the mantispid will shuffle across to live for a time on the cannibal. Mantispids will also transfer from a male to a female when two spiders mate.

When the spider deposits an egg sac, the mantispid crawls in and begins to suck juices from inside the eggs.

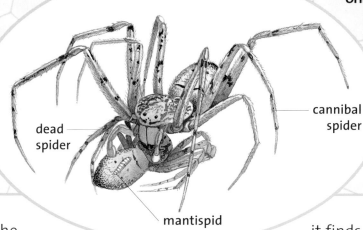

dead spider

cannibal spider

mantispid

◀ *A mantispid larva crawls from a cannibalized spider.*

the organs of the prey. The robber fly then sucks out the soup of **liquefied** insect guts. Robber flies are very messy eaters, though. Some other insects feed on the dribbles of insect soup that run down the mouth of a robber fly as it feeds. Rather than wait around for free food, some of these food thieves let the robber fly carry them from meal to meal.

One type of tiny jackal fly rides from place to place by clinging to the body of a much larger robber fly. The jackal fly sits between the robber fly's wings. When the robber fly catches another insect, it finds a perch and begins to feed. The little jackal fly then sneaks forward onto the head of the robber fly and drinks from the oozing soup of insect flesh and organs.

KEY FACTS

■ Jackal flies are named for their habit of hanging around predators waiting for scraps—just like the doglike jackals of the African grasslands.

■ Just like mantises, adult mantispids catch prey using their long, grasping front legs.

■ Blister beetles release an oily substance when alarmed. This can cause painful blisters on a person's skin, for which these insects are named.

Food **SNATCHERS**

It is often said that there is no such thing as a free meal. Unless you are a kleptoparasite, that is. These sneaky creatures steal food from the claws, webs, stomachs, and mouths of other animals. Read on to discover how these thieves manage to commit the perfect crime.

20

Rather than spending time and effort catching their own food, some animals steal things to eat from other animals. Creatures that feed like this are called **kleptoparasites.** Several types of seabirds are kleptoparasitic. These thieves harass their **hosts** until they drop or **regurgitate** (throw up) any food they are carrying.

Sick stealers

Jaegers are large, gull-like seabirds. They frequently attack smaller seabirds and try to steal their catch from them. Puffins are regular victims of jaeger raids. The small puffins catch fish and return to their burrows on land, where they regurgitate the fish for their chicks to eat. The jaegers wait for the puffins to catch the fish. Then they swoop down and attack the puffins, usually by grabbing their wingtips and turning them over so they crash into the ocean. To get away, the puffins often regurgitate their fish. This makes them lighter and better able to fly to safety. The jaegers get an easy meal by catching the regurgitated food in midair before it reaches the sea.

▼ *Airborne piracy: an Arctic jaeger attacks a kittiwake, hoping to force the gull to eject the tasty contents of its stomach.*

Flying pirates

Perhaps the most famous seabird pirates are the frigate birds. These magnificent birds have a wingspan of up to 3.5 feet (103 cm) and live in warm parts of the Pacific and Indian oceans. The feathers of most seabirds are coated with an oil that makes them waterproof. Frigate birds have little oil on their feathers, so they cannot enter the water to feed. To catch food, frigate birds sometimes skim the surface, grabbing fish and other small **prey** with their beaks. More often, these birds resort to piracy.

With their long, pointed wings, frigate birds are very agile in the air. Like jaegers, they hassle other birds until they regurgitate morsels of food. Frigate birds also harass each other. Regurgitated food may pass between many birds before it is swallowed for the final time. Frigate birds even steal prey from tuna. Tuna chase small fish close to the ocean's surface. Before the tuna can grab the prey, frigate birds swoop down and pluck the small fish from the water.

Noddy and big beak

Noddy terns are small, dark-brown seabirds with a white patch on top of their heads. Noddy terns follow pelicans as they hunt for fish. A pelican catches food by plunging into the water with its huge bill gaping open. Water rushes into the pelican's mouth and fills a large pouch that hangs

▲ *A pair of Christmas Island frigate birds harass a brown booby. The booby may be forced to regurgitate some food so it can escape.*

beneath the bill. This pouch can hold up to 3.5 gallons (13 liters) of water and fish. A noddy tern waits for the pelican to fill its pouch before landing on the head or bill of the pelican. When the pelican opens its bill, the noddy tern tries to steal fish from inside the pouch.

Sneaky thieves

Not all kleptoparasites harass other animals until they drop their food. Some are clever thieves that wait until food is unguarded before stealing it. Spiders that store prey in their webs and bees and wasps that store food in burrows are all common victims. Jackal flies are expert thieves. Many species follow **predatory** assassin bugs, mantises, and spiders. After the predator has caught a meal, the jackal fly sneaks in and feeds, too.

Crime doesn't pay

Spiderwebs are a rich source of food for many kleptoparasites. Not all these robbers get away with their crimes, however. Some get eaten by their potential

▼ *A noddy tern prepares to land on the beak of a feeding pelican.*

▲ *The chloropid flies perched around—and on—this mantis will sneak in closer to steal morsels of mantis food.*

23

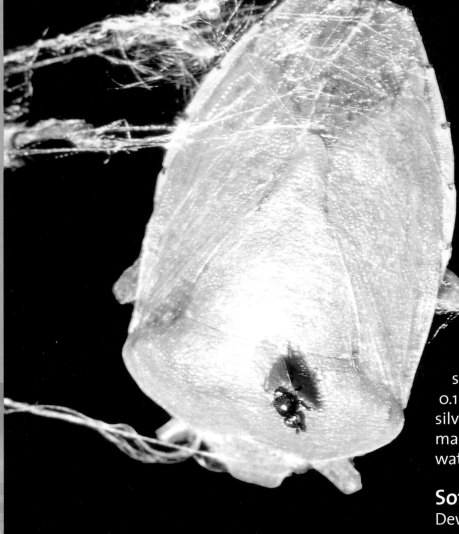

attract jackal flies. The flies follow the smell until they find the spider and its prey. The flies then begin to feed on **liquefied** shield bug organs dribbled by the spider. Some kleptoparasites are even braver and actually live on spiderwebs for the sole purpose of stealing food. Many large spiders share their webs with much smaller spiders. These guests are called dewdrop spiders. Measuring around 0.1 inches (3 mm) long, the silvery bodies of dewdrop spiders make them look like tiny drops of water glistening on the web.

Softly, softly

Dewdrop spiders move slowly and carefully around the web, to which they remain attached at all times by a safety line of silk. If the owner of the web detects the little thief, the dewdrop spider can drop from the web and hang from its safety line. The dewdrop spider returns to the web when the danger has passed. When the host spider catches an insect in its web, the dewdrop spider creeps up and begins feeding, too.

Getting away with it

Dewdrop spiders also steal stored prey from the web. Large spiders catch and wrap up prey in silk.

▲ *A shield bug trapped in a spiderweb releases chemicals that attract jackal flies.*

victims. Some dance flies feed on the prey of spiders while the spider itself is feeding. A dance fly walks delicately across a spiderweb. One false move, and the dance fly gets entangled in the silken threads. The trapped fly then becomes lunch for the spider.

Some kleptoparasites only arrive on spiderwebs when food is "on the table." When they are in danger, shield bugs give off smelly chemicals to try to drive enemies away. The defensive chemicals released by a shield bug trapped on a spiderweb

◀ *Jackal flies prepare to feed on a mixture of spider saliva and the liquefied organs of this crab spider's insect prey.*

▼ *A dewdrop spider dangles to safety on a silken thread as the web's owner, a female golden silk spider, closes in.*

They then attach it to the web so they can eat it later. If the dewdrop spider finds this stored food, it quickly attaches a line of silk between itself and the prey. The dewdrop spider snips away the silk attaching the prey to the web. It then carefully releases the cut ends of the web—if the dewdrop spider were to release the ends suddenly, the owner of the web would be alerted to the crime. The tiny spider then sneaks away with the stolen prey.

Wedding presents

Many animals steal from spiderwebs, but some do it for reasons other than simply getting a free meal. Scorpionflies are named for the bulb at the tip of the male's body that looks like a scorpion's stinger. This is not a true stinger, however, but a harmless structure used in mating.

For a male scorpionfly, mating can be a hazardous business. A female may try to eat the male before, during, or after mating. So, the male presents the female with a present, or **nuptial gift,** before mating.

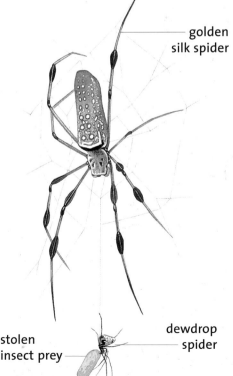

golden silk spider

stolen insect prey

dewdrop spider

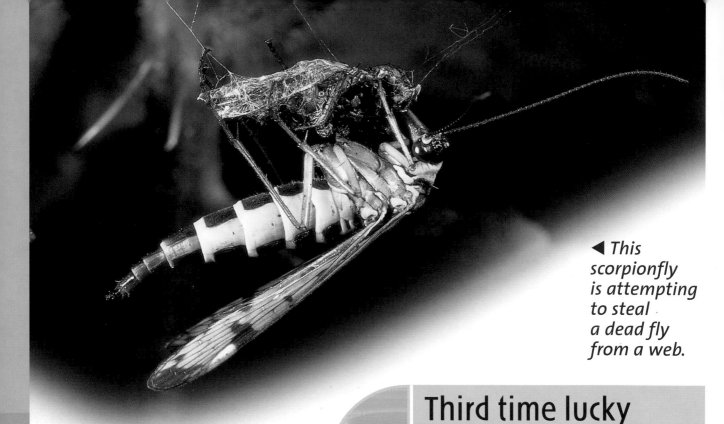

◄ This scorpionfly is attempting to steal a dead fly from a web.

This keeps her busy while the male mates with her before escaping unharmed.

The nuptial gift is usually a dead insect, and the males often steal these from spiderwebs. Scorpionflies move easily across the surface of a web. If they get tangled up, they release a brown fluid from their mouths that dissolves the spider silk.

After stealing a dead insect from a web, the male scorpionfly carries his loot to a safe place. He then releases a chemical that attracts females, and waits for their arrival. Other male scorpionflies can detect this chemical, though,

Third time lucky

Kleptoparasites often attack parasitic wasps. One species of mud-dauber wasp, for example, is attacked by three different flies, each using a different strategy. The mud-dauber wasp grabs grasshoppers and drags them to its burrow. It collects several before laying an egg. After hatching, the wasp **larva** eats the grasshoppers.

The wasp seals the burrow each time before setting off in search of its quarry. While the wasp is away, one type of fly digs away the top of the burrow and deposits a larva of its own inside. A second fly waits until the wasp returns with a grasshopper before laying a larva on it. A third fly waits until the wasp opens its burrow before laying a larva on the grasshopper inside. The kleptoparasitic fly larvae eat the grasshoppers and the wasp egg, too.

◄ A kleptoparasitic fly breaks into a wasp's burrow.

and they also fly toward the source. When these rival males arrive they check out the size of the nuptial gift. If it is big enough, many try to take the gift by force. Some males, though, use sneaky tactics to win possession of the prize. By moving their bodies in a certain way, these males pretend to be females. They trick the male into handing over his gift, before flying off.

Stealing from bees

With their rich, high-quality foods of **pollen** and **nectar,** bees are tempting targets for many kleptoparasites. For example, tiny flies called bee lice live on the bodies of honeybees. When they are hungry, the bee lice crawl up to the bee's head. This irritates the bee, which regurgitates a small drop of sweet nectar. The bee lice then thrust their mouthparts into the bee's mouth to draw out the sugary liquid.

27

Honeybees live in large **colonies** with thousands of workers, but most bees live alone. These solitary bees are also at risk from food thieves. The bees make nest chambers that they fill with pollen for their **larvae** to feed on. These stores of food may be attacked by several types of kleptoparasites. The thieves attack the chamber while the resident bee is away collecting pollen. Some *Osmia* bee nests, for example, are

▲ *An* Osmia *bee at the entrance to its nest. When the bee heads off to collect pollen, the nest may be invaded by an enemy bee.*

◀ *Bee lice scamper over the body of a queen honeybee. The bee lice steal nectar from the mouths of their hosts.*

Boring kleptoparasites

Not all kleptoparasites steal food. Some rely on other species to do hard work for them. Most parasitic wasps lay their eggs in or on the larvae of other insects. The wasp larva then devours the host. *Rhysella* wasps attack the wood-feeding larvae of alder wood wasps. A female *Rhysella* walks over bark until she detects a wood wasp larva munching through the wood. The *Rhysella* uses her long egg-laying tube to bore into the wood. She lays an egg on the wood wasp and leaves, but her drilling may have been watched by another type of wasp. The young of this second wasp also feed on alder wood wasp larvae, but the adult female is unable to drill a hole of her own into the wood. Instead, she must wait for *Rhysella* to do the work for her. She forces her egg tube down the hole drilled by *Rhysella* and lays an egg. When the egg hatches, the larva kills the young *Rhysella* before feeding on the wood wasp larva.

egg tube

◀ **Rhysella** *uses its enormous egg tube to drill into wood.*

raided by kleptoparasitic bees called *Stelis*. A female *Stelis* sneaks into an *Osmia* nest and judges the amount of pollen inside. If the chamber is almost full, she makes a small pyramid of pollen and lays an egg behind it. When the *Osmia* bee returns, it cannot spot the egg hidden behind the pyramid.

Hatching and stealing

When attacking another type of *Osmia* bee, the female *Stelis* digs out a hole in the pollen. She lays an egg inside the hole before sealing it up. This hides the egg from the *Osmia* bee host.

Stelis bee larvae hatch quickly and begin feeding on the stores of pollen. The larvae also eat the young of the unsuspecting *Osmia* bee before they get a chance to hatch.

KEY FACTS

■ 45 dewdrop spiders have been seen on a single spiderweb.

■ Biologists have discovered that about half of all male scorpionflies that try to steal prey from webs are caught by the spider.

■ Some parasitic wasps can tell if grasshoppers have been parasitized and remove fly larvae with their mouthparts.

28

▶ For lions, stealing food from smaller predators is much safer than tackling dangerous prey animals.

Bigger and stronger

People usually think of lions as fearless predators that tackle wildebeest, zebras, and antelope. But lions are also kleptoparasites that steal food from smaller predators. Rather than using stealthy tactics, lions simply use brute force and weight of numbers to chase cheetahs or hyenas away from their kills.

Hyenas also profit from the hard work of others. They can have a serious impact on populations of African wild dogs. A successful hunt for the dogs can take up a lot of time and energy. To lose the fruits of a long chase to hyenas can be disastrous for these predators.

When predators such as a pride of lions make a kill on the African grasslands, kleptoparasites are soon on the scene to steal scraps. Jackals and vultures grab what they can while keeping just out of range of the predators. Once the lions leave the **carcass,** the thieves swiftly devour the last of the victim's remains.

▼ A variety of vultures compete to steal scraps of flesh from a carcass as a small group of spotted hyenas feed.

Things to Do

Checking out kleptos

With their supplies of dead insects conveniently wrapped in silk, spiderwebs are a rich source of food for **kleptoparasites.** To see kleptoparasites in action, perhaps the best places to look are the webs of female golden silk spiders.

These spiders are enormous, with orange and black bodies and legs. They often string their vast webs between stands of

◄ *A female golden silk spider usually sits at the hub of her vast web. These webs can measure more than 3 feet (1 m) across.*

trees near brooks or between forest clearings. When you go looking for these spiders, make sure you take an adult with you. Do not disturb the spiders in any way because they can give a nasty bite. Look closely at the web and you will see that the golden silk spider keeps her food stash near the center, or hub, of her web. Why do you think she does this?

Golden silk spiders are often plagued by dewdrop spiders. These thieves snatch unguarded food from the web, and also feed on trapped insects that are too small for their **hosts** to bother with. Dewdrop spiders are tiny, but their bright white bodies make them easy to spot. When you locate one, see if you can find the spider's silken safety line.

Books and websites

■ Levi, Herbert W. and Lorna R. Levi. *Spiders and their Kin.* New York: St. Martin's Press, 2001.

■ Fowler, Allan. *Seeing Seabirds* Danbury, Connecticut: Children's Press, 2000.

■ *Learn about lions at* http://www.africanlions.org

■ *Loads of insect fun at* http://www.insectlore.com

30

Words to Know

arachnid
Animal group that includes spiders, mites, ticks, and scorpions

bivouac
Temporary nest constructed by army ants

cannibalize
When an animal eats another member of its own species (type)

carcass
Dead body of an animal

colony
Group of insects that live together, such as ants

commensalism
Relationship between two creatures in which one benefits but the other is unaffected

forage
To search for food

host
Animal or plant that supports a parasite or commensal organism

kleptoparasite
Animal that feeds by stealing from other creatures

larva
Young of an insect such as a fly (plural: larvae)

liquefy
To break something down into a liquid

mutualism
Relationship between two creatures in which both partners benefit

nectar
Sugary liquid produced by plants to reward pollinators

nuptial gift
Gift given by a male to a female (or vice versa) before mating takes place

ootheca
Egg sac of insects like mantises and cockroaches

organism
Any type of living thing, such as plants and animals

parasite
Organism that benefits at the expense of another

phoresy
Symbiosis in which one partner hitches a ride from place to place on the other

pollen
Male sex cells of plants; pollen forms a fine dust inside flowers

predator
Animal that eats other animals

prey
Animal that is caught and eaten by a predator

pupate
To change from an insect larva into an adult

regurgitate
To throw up food

symbiosis
Close relationship between different types of creatures (plural: symbioses)

Index

Numbers in *italics* refer to pictures

32

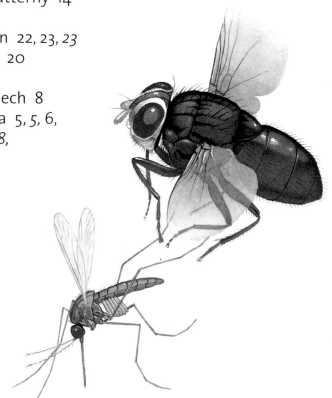